D0535083

Dimorphodon

Written by Rupert Oliver
Illustrated by Roger Payne

© 1986 Rourke Enterprises, Inc.

All rights reserved. No part of this book may be reproduced or utilized in any form or by any means, electronic or mechanical including photocopying, recording or by any information storage and retrieval system without permission in writing from the publisher.

Library of Congress Cataloging in Publication Data

Oliver, Rupert.
  Dimorphodon.

  Summary: Follows a flying dinosaur through her day as she glides on air currents, searches for food, and observes many of the other inhabitants of her prehistoric world.
  1. Dimorphodon—Juvenile literature.   [1. Dimorphodon. 2. Dinosaurs]   I. Payne, Roger, ill.   II. Title.
QE862.P7O45   1986   567.9'7   85-28341
ISBN 0-86592-217-9

Rourke Enterprises, Inc.
Vero Beach, FL 32964

Dimorphodon

Dilophosaurus

Brachiosaurus

Lystrosaurus

Rutiodon

Dimorphodon

Mamenchisaurus

Plateosaurus

Chasmosaurus

Protoceratops

The roar shattered the dawn stillness of the forest and echoed from tree to tree. The noise of crashing branches and thudding footsteps startled every animal in the forest and set dozens of small animals running for cover. High in the branches of a tree Dimorphodon woke from her sleep with a start. There was something happening, and it might be dangerous.

She twisted to look in the direction of all the noise. Just at that moment the bushes were smashed apart and two large animals tumbled into view. One was a Scelidosaurus, normally a quiet plant eater, but the other was a Megalosaurus which hunted and ate other dinosaurs. While Scelidosaurus was trying to escape, Megalosaurus was attacking viciously.

Dimorphodon realized that the struggling dinosaurs were no threat to her, but she kept a wary eye on them just in case. Before long the Megalosaurus clawed the hind leg of Scelidosaurus and brought it down. There was still plenty of fight left in the plant eater, and its bony back kept the meat eater at bay for some time. Eventually, Megalosaurus dug his teeth into Scelidosaurus' neck and the plant eater moved no more.

Megalosaurus had no sooner begun to eat his meal than a pair of Sarcosaurs appeared. They had been attracted by the fight and the smell of blood. Perhaps they would be able to scavenge a meal after Megalosaurus had eaten its fill.

While Megalosaurus gorged itself on the Scelidosaurus, Dimorphodon dropped from her branch and flew away. First she headed for the cliffs along the seashore, where there were usually gusts of wind blowing upwards. If she could find an updraft it would save her a tiring flight.

Dimorphodon soon reached the cliffs beside the sparkling ocean and flew around trying to find an updraft. As soon as she found one, Dimorphodon began to circle tightly. She did not need to flap her wings for the wind was blowing her upwards. As soon as she reached a good height Dimorphodon would turn inland and glide in search of food.

The wind carried Dimorphodon higher and higher into the clear blue sky. Dimorphodon was just getting ready to turn inland when the wind changed. The shift in direction was so sudden that Dimorphodon was caught unawares. The new, strong wind tumbled her over and over in the air. Dimorphodon felt herself falling through the air and it was some time before she could regain her balance.

By the time Dimorphodon had been able to steady herself and begin to fly properly, she was in a strong violent wind. That wind was blowing her out to sea, away from the land. Dimorphodon tried climbing higher, but the wind was just as strong and was still blowing her out to sea. Then she dove down toward the shimmering ocean. At just above wave-top height Dimorphodon pulled out of her dive. Down here the wind was less strong and she could make headway toward the distant shore.

Dimorphodon beat her wings rhythmically as she flew along. Occasionally her wings would dip into the ocean and Dimorphodon nearly lost control. If she plunged into the sea Dimorphodon was not sure if she would be able to get airborne again. Then Dimorphodon became aware of some dark shapes beneath the water. They were moving in the same direction as she was and they were swimming very quickly. Suddenly one of them jumped completely out of the water and then plunged back again with a tremendous splash.

Dimorphodon veered off to one side in alarm. Then another of the creatures jumped from the ocean. This time Dimorphodon got a clear look at it and realized that it was an ichthyosaur and that she had nothing to fear from this creature.

Then Dimorphodon found herself near the coast. This time she did not use the air currents of the cliffs to gain height. Instead she flew a little way inland and then began to climb under her own power. As she gradually gained height she passed over a mixed herd of dinosaurs.

The herd were Ohmdenosaurs. These dinosaurs were plant eaters which fed off the many trees and ferns in the area. From Dimorphodon's vantage point, high in the air, she could see something that the dinosaurs could not. Just behind one group of plants was resting a Metriacanthosaurus. If the plant eaters got too close, the Metriacanthosaurus might attack them.

As Dimorphodon cruised on across the landscape she kept a keen eye open for food. For a long time she could see nothing. Then her sharp eyes spotted something moving down by the river. It was a small mammal which had crept out for a drink. Dimorphodon adjusted her wings correctly and then plunged down out of the sky.

Her dive was swift, short and accurate. Within seconds her claws had closed around the mammal and her jaws had snuffed the life out of the little creature. Dimorphodon could eat for the first time that day.

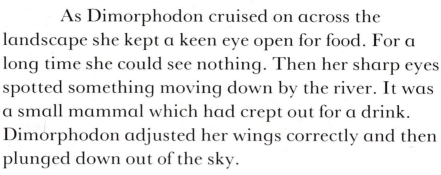

Suddenly, the waters of the river thrashed apart and and a long scaly head emerged from the waters. The head was swiftly followed by a powerful body and Dimorphodon recognized it as belonging to a crocodile. Dimorphodon was not very quick at taking off from the ground, but danger was threatening. Desperately, she fluttered her wings and scrambled to take off into the air.

She kept hold of the mammal which she had
killed and was just becoming airborne when the
crocodile arrived. An extra strong flap of her wings
carried Dimorphodon into the air and the jaws of the
crocodile snapped shut just inches beneath her.

With her kill securely grasped in her mouth, Dimorphodon flew back to the upper branches of the forest and roosted. There she ate her fill of the tiny mammal. When she had finished her meal Dimorphodon realized that it was getting late and the shadows were beginning to lengthen. Soon it would be night. Dimorphodon moved to a more comfortable and secure branch on the tree. There she closed her eyes and fell asleep.

Dimorphodon and Early Jurassic Europe

Later types of pterosaur

Pterodactylus

Pteranodon

The days of Dimorphodon

By studying rocks, scientists have been able to divide the entire history of the world into four great eras: the Precambrian, the Paleozoic, the Mesozoic and the Cenozoic. Dimorphodon lived during the fourth period, the Mesozoic which means "middle life". The Mesozoic began about 225 million years ago and ended about 65 million years ago. This great era is itself divided into the three periods, the Triassic, the Jurassic and the Cretaceous. Dimorphodon fossils have been found in the earliest rocks of the Jurassic. This means that the reptile lived about 190 million years ago.

The flying reptiles

Dimorphodon was not a dinosaur. It belonged to a group of reptiles known today as Pterosauria. However, the Pterosauria came under the much larger group of reptiles which is known as the Archosaurs. Archosaur means "ruling reptiles" and it is a very apt name for it is one of the largest of all reptile groups. It includes not only the flying reptiles of millions of years ago but also the crocodiles of today, the extinct Aetosaurs and Phytosaurs and most important of all the dinosaurs. The line which

led to the flying reptiles diverged from the other Archosaurs some time during the Triassic period, that is some 210 million years ago. No fossils have been found of animals which are partly Pterosaur and partly land reptiles. The earliest known fossil is Dimorphodon and this is already a fully developed Pterosaur. However, the later evolution of the Pterosaurs is well recorded by scientists. It is clear that Dimorphodon, with its heavy head and long, bony tail, was a fairly primitive flying reptile. In the course of evolution the Pterosaurs gained smaller heads, which made flying easier, and lost their tails, which meant they could maneuver much more accurately. All the Pterosaurs died out at the end of the Mesozoic, at the same time as the dinosaurs.

The land of Dimorphodon

The fossils of Dimorphodon have been found in England. But 190 million years ago England was very different from today. Perhaps the most noticeable difference would have been the plant life. There were no trees as we know them and no grass at all. Nor were there any flowering plants for they had not yet evolved. The plants which dominated the land were the tall cordates, tree ferns and primitive conifers which can be seen in the story. Other plants included ferns, horsetails, cycads and cycadeoids. Some of these plants can still be found in England, but they are much rarer than they were 190 million years ago, and others have disappeared entirely.

Early Jurassic animals

The time in which Dimorphodon lived was part of the "Age of the Dinosaurs", yet most of the dinosaurs familiar to dinosaur experts had not yet evolved. It was only a few million years earlier that the dinosaurs had first appeared and there had not yet appeared the bewildering variety of creatures with which we are so familiar. Perhaps the best known dinosaur of the period and place was Megalosaurus. This 30 foot long meat eater was one of the first dinosaurs ever to be discovered by scientists. In fact, it was found before anybody knew there had been dinosaurs at all and its bones created quite a sensation. When alive, it was one of the most powerful hunters in the world and must have been a terrifying sight. The Sarcosaurs, which in our story, appear to scavenge from Megalosaurus' kill, were members of the same family of dinosaurs, but were only about 11 feet long. The other hunter in the story, Metriacanthosaurus, was unusual in that it had a row of spines along its back which is thought to have supported a flap of skin. Why Metriacan-

thosaurus needed such a large flap of skin is unclear. Perhaps it was used for display, like the tail of today's peacock, or perhaps it cooled the dinosaur in hot weather. Scelidosaurus was another strange dinosaur. It had strong, bone studs all along its back and sides. These must have given the dinosaur some kind of protection against the attacks of hunters such as Megalosaurus and Metriacanthosaurus. It is possible that the Scelidosaur family evolved into the more famous Stegosaurus many years later. The future belonged to the family of which Ohmdenosaurus was a member; the Sauropods. Though Ohmdenosaurus was only about 13 feet long, later Sauropods would grow to be the largest dinosaurs ever, including the famous Brontosaurus, Diplodocus and Brachiosaurus. There were many other kinds of reptile alive at the time. One of these was the crocodile which was a member of the Archosaur group. The Ichthyosaur, on the other hand, was not an Archosaur. Nobody is really sure how the Ichthyosaur evolved for there are no fossils showing a reptile part way between a land reptile and the Ichthyosaur. However it was a very successful type of reptile and developed into many different species. Today, mammals are the most important type of land animal. Man is a mammal and so are most of the larger land animals, from a mouse to an elephant. During the days of the Dimorphodon, however, mammals were unimportant, and the few species that existed were only about the size of the creature captured by Dimorphodon.

The different structures of a bird's and Dimorphodon's wing

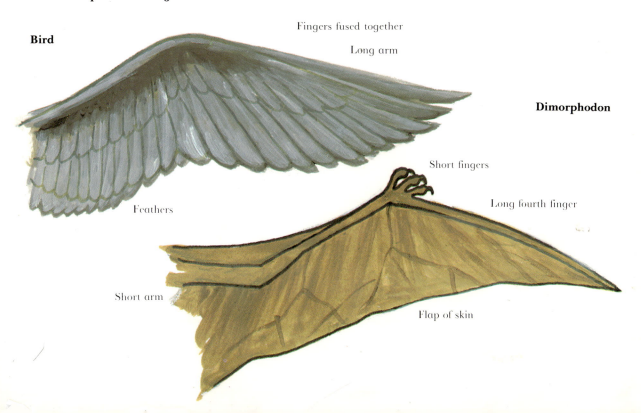

Bird

Fingers fused together

Long arm

Dimorphodon

Short fingers

Long fourth finger

Feathers

Short arm

Flap of skin